Clothes Around the World

Belts, Bags and Jewellery

Jane Bingham

WAYLAND

First published in 2008 by Wayland

Copyright © Wayland 2008

Wayland
338 Euston Road
London NW1 3BH

Wayland Australia
Level 17/207 Kent Street
Sydney NSW 2000

Senior editor: Joyce Bentley
Designer: Holly Fullbrook
Picture researcher: Kathy Lockley

British Library Cataloguing in Publication Data
Bingham, Jane
        Bags, belts and jewellery. - (Clothes around the world)
        1. Dress accessories - Juvenile literature
        I. Title
        391.4'4

ISBN 978 0 7502 5312 3

Picture acknowledgements:
Art Archive/British Library: 11; Art Archive/Musee du Chateau de Versailles/Gianni Dagli Orti: 12; Bettmann/Corbis: 13;Corbis: 7; Construction Photogaphy/Corbis: 20; Dinodia Images/Alamy: 1, 26; DLILLC/Corbis: 9; Angela Fisher/Robert Estall Photo Agency/Alamy: 25; Natalie Forbes/Corbis: 21; Tim Graham/Corbis: 24; Jeff Greenberg/Alamy: 19; Roberto Herrett/Alamy: 22; Chris Howes/Wild Places Photography/Alamy: 18; Rainer Jahns/Alamy: 14; John Kershaw/Alamy: 16; Viviane Moos/Corbis: 27; Photo Japan/Alamy: 6; Rex Features: 5; Bill Ross/Corbis: 23; Smithsonian Institution/Corbis: 17; Kristen Soper/Alamy: 4; Penny Tweedie/Panos Pictures: 8; Visual Arts Library (London)/Alamy: 10; Andrew Woodley/Alamy: 3, 15

Printed in China

Wayland is a division of Hachette Children's Books, an Hachette Livre UK company.

Contents

Why do people wear belts, bags and jewellery?

People have worn belts, bags and jewellery for thousands of years. These items of clothing don't just look great. They have many uses too.

Belts are very important. Without a belt, some of your clothes would fall down round your knees! A belt can also provide a very useful place to hang things from.

Everyone needs bags to carry things. Many people have a bag to hold small objects like money and keys. Bags are also useful for carrying large, heavy things, such as books.

It Works!

Bags on belts
Some people have bags fixed onto their belts. These useful bags free your hands to hold other things when you are **hiking**.

Wearing jewellery makes you look good. Your jewellery can also tell people things about you. For example, wearing a wedding ring shows that someone is married.

Belts, bags and jewellery are sometimes called **accessories**. This is another word for extras. But belts, bags and jewellery are not really extras. They are an important part of what we wear.

Accessories can make a big difference to an outfit.

Belts, bags and jewellery around the world

All around the world, people wear accessories. These items can vary from culture to culture. Each country has its own **traditional** belts, bags and jewellery.

Japanese people fasten their traditional robes with a wide belt. This belt is called an obi and it is made from a long length of silk. The silk is wound tightly round the body and tied at the back with a very large knot.

A Japanese obi is made from decorated silk. Some women carry a bag to match their obi.

Useful belt

Some Mexican farmers wear a very useful belt, called a mecapal. It is made from a wide strip of cloth, and its ends are fastened together with cords. When farmers need to carry a bundle of wood, they use their belt. They tie the cords from the belt tightly round the bundle. Then they place the strip of cloth across their forehead.

In Scotland, some men wear a narrow belt, with a small leather bag hanging down at the front. The bag is called a **sporran**, and it is used for holding money. Sporrans are worn with Scottish **kilts**.

The Aboriginal people of Australia weave bags from **reeds**. The bags are known as dilly bags and they are made in many different sizes. Dilly bags are often used for carrying food. Sometimes people use a dilly bag as a trap to catch fish.

This Aboriginal leader wears a dilly bag for a **ceremony**. The bag reminds his people of their **ancestors**.

In northwest India, women wear masses of heavy silver jewellery. As well as necklaces, bracelets, and rings, most women wear earrings and nose studs. Some women also have anklets round their ankles and rings on their toes.

The Masai people of East Africa make necklaces from colourful beads. Some women wear up to 100 different necklaces round their neck at once. The Masai also use beads to make hats, belts and bags.

Masai bead necklaces are very heavy to wear. But they look wonderful!

The history of belts, bags and jewellery

Men and women have been wearing jewellery for thousands of years. The early cave dwellers made necklaces from bones, shells and seeds. They also wore simple belts made from strips of leather .

The ancient Egyptians wore very wide necklaces that looked like collars. Egyptians also wore colourful headdresses, necklaces and belts. Some of them carried bags made from reeds.

The ancient Egyptians had very plain clothes and magnificent accessories.

Roman women loved to wear necklaces and earrings, and both men and women wore lots of rings. Even Roman children wore rings.

In **medieval times**, belts were very important. Men and women often had a money pouch attached to their belt. Knights usually wore a narrow leather belt. Hanging from the knight's belt was a **scabbard** to hold his sword.

Posy bags

Medieval men and women were very frightened of a terrible illness called the plague. They tried to keep themselves safe by carrying a posy bag. Posy bags were small bags filled with sweet-smelling herbs. People believed that the smell of the herbs would drive away the plague!

These knights are having their swords fitted into their scabbards.

The Inca people lived in South America in the 1300s. Inca warriors wore golden ornaments on their chest. They also wore large earplugs, made from gold. Inca messengers carried their messages in a small bag with a handle.

By the 1700s, women in Europe carried small, cloth bags. The bags had a drawstring at the top, so they could hang from a lady's arm.

Flashback

Earrings for men
In **Tudor times**, it was the fashion for men to wear an earring in one ear. Now, earrings for men are popular again. Some men wear a single earring, just like they did in Tudor times.

In the First World War, soldiers carried **canvas** kit bags on their backs. Kit bags were fastened with a drawstring and they contained the soldiers' clothes and equipment. Soldiers also had shoulder bags, made from leather or strong canvas cloth.

In their shoulder bags, soldiers carried a metal water bottle, and a mug, knife, fork and spoon. If they were lucky they also carried some food.

What are bags made from?

For thousands of years, people have made bags from straw, reeds and grasses. These materials can be dyed different colours, and they can be woven into all sorts of shapes. Some straw bags are firm and keep their shape. Others are soft and **flexible**.

What Would You Use?

You need a bag to carry wet, heavy soil. What would you choose?

A. A tightly woven straw basket

B. A canvas bag

C. A string bag

D. A plastic bag

(Answer on page 31)

Straw is an excellent material for bags – and for hats too!

Many bags are made from cloth. Cotton canvas is a good choice for shopping bags, because it is very strong. Some evening bags are made from rich materials, such as silk and velvet.

Leather is an excellent material for bags because it is strong and waterproof. But now bags are often made from plastic. Plastic is waterproof and easy to keep clean, and it can be any colour you like.

Rajasthan in northern India is famous for its colourful, decorated bags.

Bags are often covered with decorations. They can be decorated with **embroidery,** beads, mirrors or pieces of fabric.

What are belts and jewellery made from?

Belts can be made from cotton, wool or silk. They can also be made from rope, grass or metal. But one of the best materials for belts is leather. Leather belts are strong but flexible, and they usually last for many years.

Some belts are made from a stretchy, elastic material. They are very comfortable to wear.

These belts come from the island of Bali. They are woven from beads, seeds and shells.

Jewellery is often made from gold and silver. It can also be made from natural materials, such as leather, seeds, shells and bones.

Some jewellers use precious stones, such as diamonds, rubies and sapphires. But beads are also very important in jewellery. People make beads from glass, wood, plastic or clay.

Recently, plastic has become a very popular material for jewellery. Some designers use a clear plastic, known as Perspex, to make stunning earrings and rings.

It Doesn't Work!

Ripping earrings

Large metal earrings look dramatic, but they are very heavy to wear. When people wear very heavy earrings, their earlobes can get badly torn.

Only a millionaire could afford this stunning brooch made of emeralds and diamonds.

Useful bags

People use bags every day. They take a bag when they go to work, or to school. They use a bag for shopping, and they pack their clothes in a bag when they travel. Many people also carry a handbag. How many bags do you have at home?

Baby papoose
In the Andes mountains of South America, people have to walk very long distances. They carry their babies in a papoose on their back. A papoose is a kind of bag made from strong woven cloth. It is comfortable to wear, and it keeps the baby very close to the parent.

Rucksacks have many pockets for storing things, such as maps and drinks.

Some bags are designed for a special purpose. When people go hiking, they carry everything they need in a rucksack. Rucksacks have a very light frame. They also have straps that can be adjusted, to make the rucksack comfortable to wear.

People who play a lot of sport keep their clothes and equipment in a sports bag. Sports bags come in many shapes, to fit different kinds of equipment.

This sports bag is specially designed for tennis players. It has room for several tennis rackets.

Useful belts

Belts do a great job of holding up skirts and trousers, but they have other uses too. Belts can be used for carrying things. Sometimes, wearing a special belt can save a person's life.

Carpenters wear a wide, leather tool belt round their waist. The belt has loops for hammers and screwdrivers, and pockets for nails and screws. When carpenters wear a tool belt, they have all the tools they need close at hand. They also have their hands free to get on with their work.

Carpenters' belts are made from very strong leather. They have **compartments** for different kinds of tools.

People who work on high buildings often wear a special safety belt. The belt has a strap with a strong metal clip. The clip is attached to a safe place, so the wearer cannot fall very far.

Wearing a safety belt keeps people safe while they work.

Bags and belts for fun

Some bags and belts are really fun. They can come in a great range of colours, and they can be decorated in amazing ways.

There are lots of fun bags to choose from. Bags can be covered in pictures and patterns. They can also be completely clear, so you can see everything inside.

There are bags that look like a smiley face, a flowerpot, or even a dinosaur!

It Works!

Juice carton bags
In the Philippines, some people have found a way to recycle their empty juice cartons. Instead of throwing the cartons away, they make them into colourful bags. The bags look really fun, and they are good for the environment too.

Some fun backpacks look like a spaceman's pack.
Some look like a furry monkey clinging on to your back.

An exciting belt can brighten up your clothes
and surprise your friends. There are belts with big,
shiny buckles, and belts with amazing patterns and
designs. There are even belts fitted with tiny lights
that flash on and off!

Some girls like to wear pretty belts – and some go for something more dramatic.

Special jewellery

People wear jewellery for many different reasons.
They may want to show how wealthy they are.
Or they may wish to show their beliefs.
Jewellery can tell you a lot about a person.

Sometimes, jewellery has a religious meaning. Some Christians wear a necklace with a cross as a sign of their religion. Some Jews wear a Star of David.

When the British Queen wears the **Crown Jewels**, she is showing her very important role in society.

It Works!

Medical bracelets

Some people wear a medical bracelet as a way of keeping safe. The bracelet shows that they have a medical condition, such as an **allergy** to nuts. In an emergency, a doctor will know how to treat them – even if they are too ill to speak.

Men and boys who belong to the Sikh religion wear a simple bangle on their wrist.

Today, many people wear a coloured wristband as a sign of their beliefs.

Jewellery is often a sign of wealth. The Fulani women of North Africa wear large gold earrings to show their family's wealth. As a woman grows richer, she wears larger and larger earrings.

This Fulani woman has heavy gold earrings. She also wears large amber beads in her hair.

Jewellery for celebrations and fun

When it's time to celebrate, many people like to put on jewellery. Some people wear precious jewellery. Others choose a necklace or some earrings just because they look attractive.

Brides often wear special jewellery for their wedding. In some parts of India, the family of the bride gives her presents of jewellery. Then she wears all her gifts on her wedding day.

Indian brides wear lots of wedding jewellery. They also decorate their hands with henna patterns.

Jewellery doesn't have to be expensive. Many women wear necklaces and bracelets made from large, colourful beads. There are also some amazing earrings to choose from. They can look like butterflies, parrots, or even bananas!

Weird and Wonderful

Punk jewellery

In the 1970s, punk rockers started a new fashion in jewellery. Some of them wore safety pins through their noses. Some had metal spikes in their ears, noses and lips. They also wore heavy collars, known as chokers.

Make a sporran

This small bag is similar to a sporran – the bag that Scotsmen wear hanging from their belts. But this bag is not going on a belt. It can fit snugly in your pocket, and you can use it to hold an MP3 player.

You will need
felt ★ scissors ★ a button ★ a blunt needle ★ a pencil ★ thread ★ fun fur ★ tassels

1. Cut out a piece of felt that will wrap around your MP3 player one and a half times and is 4 cm wider than the player. Cut one end of the felt into a round shape.

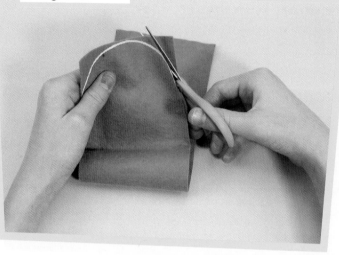
Figure 1

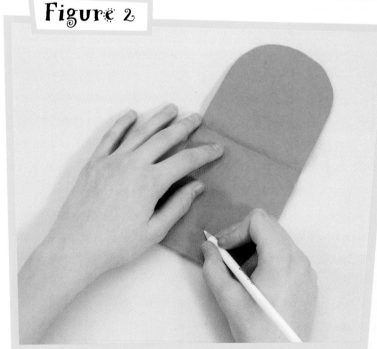
Figure 2

2. Fold the felt over, leaving the top as a flap. Mark a position for the button. Sew on the button.

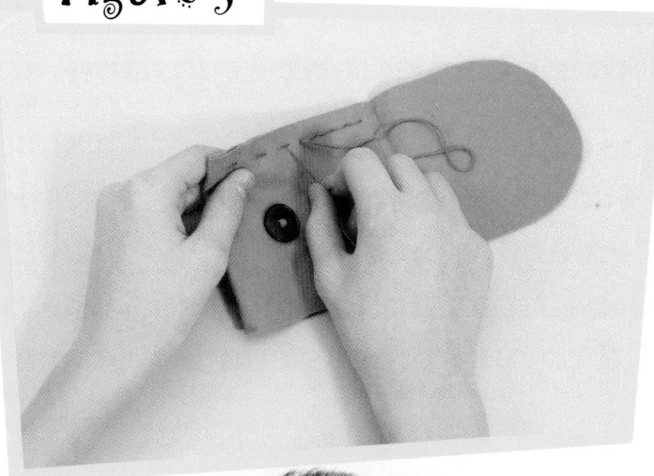

3. Use a running stitch to sew up one side of the bag. Turn back and sew the running stitch in between the other stitches, to make it strong. Now sew up the other side in the same way.

Figure 3

4. Fold down the flap and mark where it meets the button. Cut a small hole to make the button hole.

Figure 4

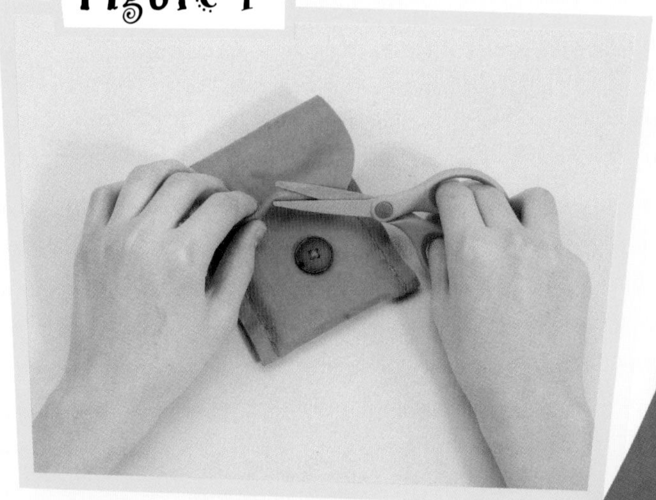

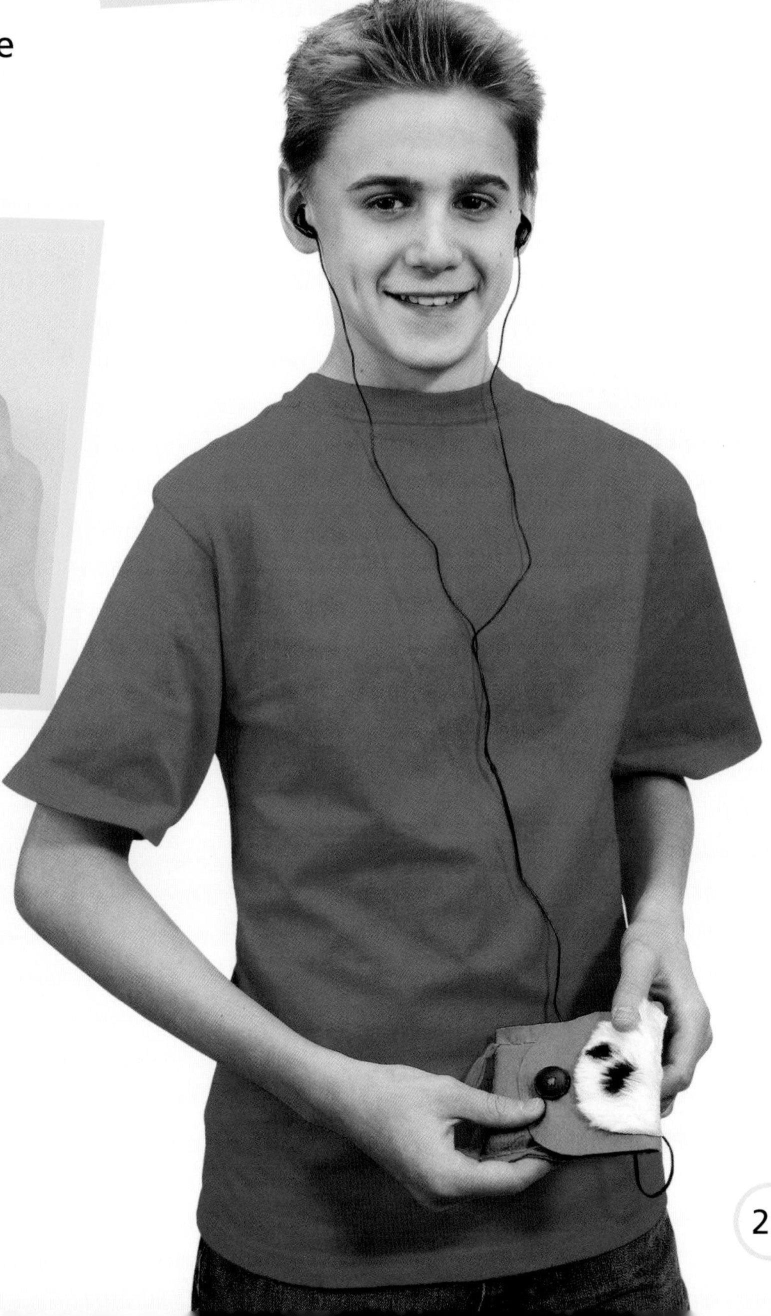

Sew on the fur and tassels to decorate the bag. Now your bag is ready to use.

Dress-up box

5-minute ancient Egyptian.

The ancient Egyptians wore a simple tunic with lots of colourful jewellery. Men and women wore wide collars made from strings of beads. They also had colourful belts and headbands.

To create your own ancient Egyptian costume, you will need a big T-shirt, and as many beads and bracelets as you can find. Use two ties and a scarf for your belt and headband, and some face paints for your Egyptian make-up.

1. Wind strings of beads around your neck to make a collar.

2. Wind more beads around your arms and add some bracelets.

3. Knot one tie around your head and the other around your waist. Fold a scarf over your waistband.

4. Now use some face paints to draw on dramatic eye make-up.

Glossary

accessories – extra items of clothing, such as belts, bags and jewellery, that are worn with an outfit

allergy – a reaction by the body to something that has caused it irritation, such as nuts, pollen or dust

ancestor – a person who has died who is related to someone who is living

canvas – very strong, thick cotton

ceremony – words, actions and/or music to mark a special occasion

compartments – separate areas that make a whole

Crown Jewels – the crown, necklace and other jewels worn by a ruler for important ceremonies

earlobe – the flap of skin at the bottom of your ear

embroidery – a design or a picture sewn on to material

flexible – able to bend easily

hiking – walking in the countryside

kilt – a heavy skirt with pleats, worn by Scotsmen

massage – to rub someone's body firmly

medieval times – a period of history between the years 1000 and 1450

natural materials – materials that come from an animal or a plant

reeds – plants with long, hollow stems that grow near water

scabbard – a holder for a sword, that hangs down from a belt

sporran – a small leather bag worn by Scotsmen

traditional – used in the same way for hundreds of years

Tudor times – a period of English history between the years 1485 and 1603

What would you use?

Answer to the question on page 14.
The best bag to use for carrying wet soil is A – a tightly woven straw basket. Straw baskets are good for carrying soil because they are strong, and the small holes in the basket allow the extra water to drain out.

A canvas bag would soon become very wet and heavy. A plastic bag would keep all the water in and would probably break. A string bag has large holes, so all the soil would soon fall out!

Index

Photos or pictures are shown below in bold, **like this**.